First World War
and Army of Occupation
War Diary
France, Belgium and Germany

27 DIVISION
80 Infantry Brigade
King's (Shropshire Light Infantry)
2nd Battalion
1 March 1914 - 31 October 1915

WO95/2262/3

The Naval & Military Press Ltd
www.nmarchive.com
Published in association with The National Archives

Published by

The Naval & Military Press Ltd

Unit 10 Ridgewood Industrial Park,

Uckfield, East Sussex,

TN22 5QE England

Tel: +44 (0) 1825 749494

www.naval-military-press.com

www.nmarchive.com

This diary has been reprinted in facsimile from the original. Any imperfections are inevitably reproduced and the quality may fall short of modern type and cartographic standards.

© **Crown Copyright**
Images reproduced by permission of The National Archives, London, England, 2015.

Contents

Document type	Place/Title	Date From	Date To
Heading	WO95/2262/3		
Heading	27th Division 80th Infy Bde 2nd Bn K.S.L.I. Dec 1914-Oct 1915		
Heading	80th Infantry Brigade. 27th Division. (Battn. Disembarked Havre from England 21.12.14) War Diary 2nd Battn. The King's Shropshire Light Infantry. 20th December, 1914 To 31st January 1915		
War Diary	Winchester	20/12/1914	20/12/1914
War Diary	Havre	21/12/1914	22/12/1914
War Diary	Aire	23/12/1914	23/12/1914
War Diary	Blaringhem	25/12/1914	05/01/1915
War Diary	Strazeele	06/01/1915	06/01/1915
War Diary	Meteren	07/01/1915	07/01/1915
War Diary	Kroistraathoek	08/01/1915	08/01/1915
War Diary	Vormezeele	09/01/1915	10/01/1915
War Diary	Dickebusch	11/01/1915	11/01/1915
War Diary	Boescheppe	12/01/1915	13/01/1915
War Diary	Dickebusch	14/01/1915	17/01/1915
War Diary	Westoutre	18/01/1915	23/01/1915
War Diary	Dickebusch	24/01/1915	31/01/1915
Heading	80th Infantry Brigade 27th Division War Diary 2nd Battn. The King's Shropshire Light Infantry. February 1915		
War Diary	Dickebusch	01/02/1915	03/02/1915
War Diary	Zevecoten	04/02/1915	04/02/1915
War Diary	Westoutre	05/02/1915	05/02/1915
War Diary	Dickebusch	06/02/1915	21/02/1915
War Diary	Westoutre	22/02/1915	26/02/1915
War Diary	Dickebusch	26/02/1915	28/02/1915
Heading	80th Infantry Brigade 27th Division War Diary 2nd Battn. The King's Shropshire Light Infantry. March 1915		
War Diary	Dickebusch	01/03/1914	01/03/1914
War Diary	St Eloi	02/03/1914	03/03/1914
War Diary	Dickebusch	04/03/1914	04/03/1914
War Diary	St Eloi	05/03/1914	06/03/1914
War Diary	Dickebusch	07/03/1914	08/03/1914
War Diary	St Eloi	09/03/1914	11/03/1914
War Diary	Westoutre	12/03/1914	14/03/1914
War Diary	St Eloi And Dickebusch	15/03/1914	15/03/1914
War Diary	Dickebusch	16/03/1914	16/03/1914
War Diary	St Eloi	17/03/1914	18/03/1914
War Diary	Dickebusch	19/03/1914	19/03/1914
War Diary	St Eloi	20/03/1914	21/03/1914
War Diary	Kruisstraathoek	22/03/1914	22/03/1914
War Diary	Dickebusch	23/03/1914	24/03/1914
War Diary	Reninghelst	25/03/1914	31/03/1914
Heading	80th Infantry Brigade 27th Division War Diary 2nd Battn. The King's Shropshire Light Infantry. April 1915		
War Diary	Reninghelst	01/04/1915	05/04/1915

Type	Location	Start	End
War Diary	Ypres	06/04/1915	11/04/1915
War Diary	Polygon Wood	12/04/1915	14/04/1915
War Diary	Ypres	15/04/1915	17/04/1915
War Diary	Polygon Wood	18/04/1915	20/04/1915
War Diary	Belle-Warde Wood	21/04/1915	22/04/1915
War Diary	Potijze	23/04/1915	24/04/1915
War Diary	Belle-Warde Wood	25/04/1915	25/04/1915
War Diary	N. of Potijze	26/04/1915	26/04/1915
War Diary	Zonnebeke	27/04/1915	27/04/1915
War Diary	Belle-Warde Wood	28/04/1915	30/04/1915
Heading	80th Infantry Brigade 27th Division War Diary 2nd Battn. The King's Shropshire Light Infantry. May 1915		
War Diary	Belle Warde	01/05/1915	03/05/1915
War Diary	Potijze	04/05/1915	04/05/1915
War Diary	Belle Warde	05/05/1915	06/05/1915
War Diary	Potijze	07/05/1915	08/05/1915
War Diary	Railway Wood	09/05/1915	12/05/1915
War Diary	Vlamertinghe (1 1/2 Miles S East Of)	13/05/1915	15/05/1915
War Diary	Belle Warde Lake	16/05/1915	17/05/1915
War Diary	Busse Boom	18/05/1915	24/05/1915
War Diary	Ypres	25/05/1915	25/05/1915
War Diary	Whittport Farm	26/05/1915	26/05/1915
War Diary	Busse Boom	27/05/1915	31/05/1915
Heading	80th Infantry Brigade 27th Division War Diary 2nd Battn. The King's Shropshire Light Infantry. June 1915		
War Diary	Dranoutre	01/06/1915	01/06/1915
War Diary	Steenwerck	02/06/1915	02/06/1915
War Diary	Armentieres	03/06/1915	30/06/1915
Heading	80th Infantry Brigade 27th Division War Diary 2nd Battn. The King's Shropshire Light Infantry. July 1915		
War Diary	Armentieres	01/07/1915	17/07/1915
War Diary	Steenwerck	18/07/1915	31/07/1915
Heading	80th Infantry Brigade 27th Division War Diary 2nd Battn. The King's Shropshire Light Infantry. August 1915		
War Diary	Steenwerck	01/08/1915	02/08/1915
War Diary	Bois Grenier	03/08/1915	09/08/1915
War Diary	Gris-Pot	10/08/1915	16/08/1915
War Diary	Bois Grenier	17/08/1915	23/08/1915
War Diary	Gris-Pot	24/08/1915	31/08/1915
Heading	80th Infantry Brigade 27th Division War Diary 2nd Battn. The King's Shropshire Light Infantry. September 1915		
War Diary	Hallobeau	01/09/1915	14/09/1915
War Diary	Borre	15/09/1915	18/09/1915
War Diary	Froissy	19/09/1915	19/09/1915
War Diary	Cappy	20/09/1915	30/09/1915
Heading	80th Infantry Brigade 27th Division War Diary 2nd Battn. The King's Shropshire Light Infantry. October 1915		
War Diary	Cappy	01/10/1915	05/10/1915
War Diary	Froissy	06/10/1915	09/10/1915
War Diary	Cappy	10/10/1915	16/10/1915
War Diary	Morcourt	17/10/1915	20/10/1915
War Diary	Cappy	21/10/1915	25/10/1915
War Diary	Mericourt	26/10/1915	26/10/1915

War Diary	Abancourt	27/10/1915	27/10/1915
War Diary	Boves	28/10/1915	28/10/1915
War Diary	Pissy	29/10/1915	31/10/1915

W095/2262/3

27TH DIVISION
80TH INFY BDE

2ND BN K.S.L.I.
DEC 1914-OCT 1915

80th Infantry Brigade.

27th Division.

(Battn. disembarked Havre from England 21.12.14)

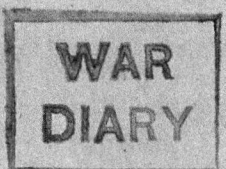

WAR DIARY

2nd BATTN. THE KING'S SHROPSHIRE LIGHT INFANTRY.

20TH DECEMBER, 1914, TO 31ST JANUARY 1915.

80th Infantry Brigade.

27th Division.

(Battn. disembarked Havre from England 21.12.14)

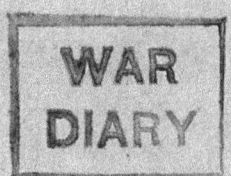

2nd BATTN. THE KING'S SHROPSHIRE LIGHT INFANTRY.

20TH DECEMBER, 1914, TO 31ST JANUARY 1915.

Army Form C. 2118.

WAR DIARY
or
INTELLIGENCE SUMMARY

(Erase heading not required.)

Instructions regarding War Diaries and Intelligence Summaries are contained in F. S. Regs., Part II. and the Staff Manual respectively. Title pages will be prepared in manuscript.

Hour, Date, Place	Summary of Events and Information	Remarks and references to Appendices
9. a. m. 20th December 1914 WINCHESTER.	The Battalion left WINCHESTER for SOUTHAMPTON by march route and embarked on S.S. Maidan same night	
21st December 1914 HAVRE	Arrived at HAVRE and disembarked about 2 p.m. Remained the night in HAVRE.	
HAVRE. 22nd December 1914	Entrained and proceeded to AIRE.	
AIRE. 23rd December 1914	Arrived and billetted at and round BLARINGHEM.	
BLARINGHEM 25th December 1914	Every Officer N.C.O. and man received a Xmas card from Their Majesties the King & Queen.	
26th December 1914	Every Officer N.C.O. and man received Princess Mary's gift.	
27th December 1914 to 31.st December 1914	Battalion engaged in digging operations	
1 st January 1915	Battalion inspected by Field Marshall Sir John French.	
2nd January 1915	Digging Operations	
3rd January 1915	Digging Operations	

Winchester Lt Colonel
Commanding 2.6 th ... Batt...

Army Form C. 2118.

WAR DIARY
or
INTELLIGENCE SUMMARY

(Erase heading not required.)

Instructions regarding War Diaries and Intelligence Summaries are contained in F.S. Regs., Part II. and the Staff Manual respectively. Title pages will be prepared in manuscript.

Hour, Date, Place	Summary of Events and Information	Remarks and references to Appendices
BLARINGHEM. 4th January 1915	March postponed owing to shortness of Boots.	
3rd January 1915	Left BLARINGHEM and marched to (from billets about) STRAZEELE. Distance 11½ (eleven and a half) miles.	
STRAZEELE 6th January 1915	Left STRAZEELE and moved into billets in neighbourhood of METEREN. Distance 3 (three) miles.	
METEREN 4th January 1915	Left METEREN and marched to KROISTRAATHOEK. Brigade went into the trenches in support to the rest of the Bde.	
KROISTRAATHOEK. 8th Jan'y 1915	Germans commenced shelling about mid-day and had to leave billets and go into trenches, dug-outs and ditches. Eventually shelled till dusk. Marched to VORMEZEELE in the evening and took over trenches just beyond village from 1st Bn. Rifle Bde. Trenches taken over correct and we suffered no casualties.	3 killed 10 wounded
VORMEZEELE. 9th January 1915	During night 8th/9th January rifle fire was going on continually. During the day most of the trenches were shelled, the worst was that being the machine gun emplacement.	1 wounded
VORMEZEELE 10th January 1915	Rifle fire during night perfect. German did not shell during the day, but Artillery shelled German trenches most of the day. Battalion relieved in the evening by the Somerset L.I. No casualties at list being relieved. Men suffered severely from wet state of trenches.	3 wounded

WAR DIARY
or
INTELLIGENCE SUMMARY

(Erase heading not required.)

Army Form C. 2118.

Instructions regarding War Diaries and Intelligence Summaries are contained in F. S. Regs., Part II. and the Staff Manual respectively. Title pages will be prepared in manuscript.

Hour, Date, Place	Summary of Events and Information	Remarks and references to Appendices
DICKEBUSCH. January 11th 1915	The communication between the trenches and Battalion Hd Qrs was found very difficult owing to wires having been cut for some time. Capt Batten Hd Qrs was about 600 yds in rear of more forward trenches. That relief from trenches Batten marched to DICKEBUSCH and billeted there.	
BOESCHEPPE January 12th 1915	Battalion marched to BOESCHEPPE and were billeted. Rested at BOESCHEPPE and men had a bath. About 300 sufferers from sore feet & frostbite and were unable to march.	
January 13th 1915	Returned to DICKEBUSCH about 500 strong having also such and some at BOESCHEPPE under command of Major E.A. Wilkinson.	
DICKEBUSCH January 14th 1915	Went into trenches in evening relieving the Duke of Cornwall L.I. The Battalion with the 1st Rifle Bde taking the centre sector [?] Brigade line. Both Battalions had their Head Qrs at LA FERME DE LA CONFLUENCE. One NCO wounded going into the trenches. Heavy rifle fire during the night.	1 Wounded
January 15th 1915	Were shelled most of the day.	
January 16th 1915	Heavy Rifle fire during the night 15/16th January 1915. Relieved in evening by 2nd Gloucester Regt, marched to DICKEBUSCH and billeted.	(Lt. ?) killed (Lt. ? wounded) (Lt. [?] Lt. E.V.T.A. SPINK wounded) [signature] Lt Colonel Commdg. 2nd Bn Shropshire L.I.

Army Form C. 2113.

WAR DIARY
or
INTELLIGENCE SUMMARY

(Erase heading not required.)

Instructions regarding War Diaries and Intelligence Summaries are contained in F. S. Regs., Part II. and the Staff Manual respectively. Title pages will be prepared in manuscript.

Hour, Date, Place	Summary of Events and Information	Remarks and references to Appendices
DICKEBUSCH January 14th 1915	Marched to WESTOUTRE but were billeted.	
WESTOUTRE January 18th 1915	Halted at WESTOUTRE until January 23rd 1915	
January 23rd 1915	Marched to DICKEBUSCH and were billeted.	
DICKEBUSCH January 24th 1915	Took over same trenches from D. Cornwall L.I.	5 Wounded
January 25th 1915	In trenches. No casualties	
January 26th 1915	Relieved by D. Cornwall L.I. and went into billets at DICKEBUSCH	
January 27th 1915	Halted at DICKEBUSCH	
January 28th 1915	Returned to trenches and relieved D. Cornwalls L.I.	
January 29th 1915	In trenches. Nine Casualties including 2nd Lt A.M. Davies wounded	2nd Lt A.M. DAVIES wounded 5 Others wounded
January 30th 1915	Relieved by 2nd Bn Gloucester Regt. Captain C.E. Atchison wounded. Marched to DICKEBUSCH & billeted	Capt. C.E. ATCHISON wounded 2 Others wounded
January 31st 1915	Took over trenches at ST. ELOI and relieved Princess Patricia's Canadian Light Infantry	

1247 W 3299 200,000 (E) 8/14 J.B.C. & A. Forms/C. 2118/11.

80th Infantry Brigade.
27th Division.

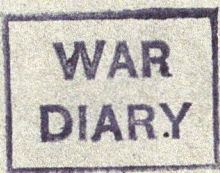

2nd BATTN. THE KING'S SHROPSHIRE LIGHT INFANTRY.

F E B R U A R Y

1 9 1 5

WAR DIARY or INTELLIGENCE SUMMARY

Army Form C. 2118.

Instructions regarding War Diaries and Intelligence Summaries are contained in F. S. Regs., Part II. and the Staff Manual respectively. Title pages will be prepared in manuscript.

(Erase heading not required.)

Hour, Date, Place	Summary of Events and Information	Remarks and references to Appendices
DICKEBUSCH February 2nd 1915	In trenches	1 killed & 2 wounded
DICKEBUSCH February 2nd 1915	Relieved by 4th A. & S. Bns and billeted in DICKEBUSCH	1 killed in billet
DICKEBUSCH February 3rd 1915	Halted at DICKEBUSCH for day.	
ZEVECOTEN February 4th 1915	Battalion left DICKEBUSCH for WESTOUTRE. Halted at ZEVECOTEN owing to report that Germans had broken through and when the night in huts.	(5th)
WESTOUTRE February 5th 1915	Left ZEVECOTEN in morning, marched to WESTOUTRE. [N.B. Sh... we had orders to stand to and it was reported that the Germans had taken a wood, but were not attacked during the night]	
February 6th, 7th, 8th 1915 DICKEBUSCH February 9th 1915	Rested in billets at WESTOUTRE Left WESTOUTRE for DICKEBUSCH and went into huts N. of DICKEBUSCH	
February 10th 1915	Went into trenches relieving 1/6th Highlanders in right sector — no casualties	1 killed
February 11th 1915	In trenches, were shelled during day but had following	2nd Lt. J.O. FARRER wounded 2 killed & 6 wounded
February 12th 1915	Relieved by 4th Rifle Bde, marched to DICKEBUSCH and occupied huts.	

[signature] 2/Lt
Commdg. 2nd Bn. Tpe of Hertfordshire [?]

Army Form C. 2118.

WAR DIARY
or
INTELLIGENCE SUMMARY

(Erase heading not required.)

Instructions regarding War Diaries and Intelligence Summaries are contained in F. S. Regs., Part II. and the Staff Manual respectively. Title pages will be prepared in manuscript.

Hour, Date, Place	Summary of Events and Information	Remarks and references to Appendices
DICKEBUSCH February 13th 1915	Halted at DICKEBUSCH. Reinforcing draft of 1 Offr & 163 other ranks joined Bn.	
February 14th 1915	Battalion should have gone into right sector but owing to situation April St Eloi we did not relieve the 10th R.Bde. We went to see night in a farm near DICKEBUSCH	
February 15th 1915	Relieved 10th R.Bde in right sector of trenches. No casualties on relief	
February 16th 1915	In trenches. No 8 trench shelled heavily and had following casualties	3 Killed 11 Wounded
February 17th 1915	In trenches. Relieved by 10th R.Bde marched to DICKEBUSCH and were billeted. A draft of 114 N.C.O.s & men arrived	2 Killed 6 Wounded
February 18th 1915	Billeted at DICKEBUSCH.	
February 19th 1915	Relieved 10th R.Bde in right sector. No casualties during relief	1 Killed
February 20th 1915	In trenches [and had following casualties]	1 Killed 2 Wounded
February 21st 1915	In trenches during day. Relieved by D.C.L.I. and marched back to DICKEBUSCH	1 Wounded
WESTOUTRE February 22nd 1915	Marched to WESTOUTRE and billeted there. A Draft of 1 Officer & 253 other ranks joined Battalion	
February 23rd 1915	Rested in billets at WESTOUTRE	

Manning Lt Col
Cmdg 2/14 S.L.I.

Army Form C. 2118.

WAR DIARY
or
INTELLIGENCE SUMMARY

(Erase heading not required.)

Instructions regarding War Diaries and Intelligence Summaries are contained in F.S. Regs., Part II. and the Staff Manual respectively. Title pages will be prepared in manuscript.

Hour, Date, Place	Summary of Events and Information	Remarks and references to Appendices
WESTOUTRE February 20th till 26th 1915	Rest in billets at WESTOUTRE	
DICKEBUSCH February 27th 1915	Marched to DICKEBUSCH and billeted	85a
February 28th 1915	In Billets at DICKEBUSCH	Month K. 10, W 1 + 3 Drafts 2+600
	21/1915 28/1915 }	
	Kennedy Lees Bn. Yeye (Shropshire L.I.)	Lieutenant Colonel

mc

80th Infantry Brigade.
27th Division.

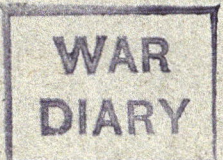

2nd BATTN. THE KING'S SHROPSHIRE LIGHT INFANTRY.

M A R C H

1 9 1 5

Army Form C. 2118.

WAR DIARY
or
INTELLIGENCE SUMMARY
(Erase heading not required.)

2nd Bn Yorks & Lancs Regt

Instructions regarding War Diaries and Intelligence Summaries are contained in F. S. Regs., Part II. and the Staff Manual respectively. Title pages will be prepared in manuscript.

Hour, Date, Place	Summary of Events and Information	Remarks and references to Appendices
MARCH 1914.		
1st. Dickebush.	Went into trenches and relieved 4th Rifle Brigade at St Eloi	1 man died of wounds, 5 men wounded
2nd. St Eloi	In trenches at St Eloi	2ndLt W.D.VIVYAN (Att 2nd Bn), Rfn F.G.BIRD - 2 men killed, 4 men wounded
3rd. St Eloi	Relieved in trenches by 4th Rifle Brigade and marched back to billets in DICKEBUSCH.	3 men killed, 4 men wounded
4th. DICKEBUSCH.	In billets at DICKEBUSCH.	
5th. St Eloi	Relieved 4th Rifle Brigade in trenches at St Eloi	2 men killed
6th. St Eloi	In trenches at St Eloi	9 men wounded
7th. DICKEBUSCH	Relieved in trenches by 4th Rifle Brigade and marched back to billets in DICKEBUSCH	6 men killed, Lieutenant W.J.BROOKE & 2ndLt A.C.P.BIDDLE-COPE, 2ndLt G.HOLMAN & 7 men wounded
8th. DICKEBUSCH.	In billets at DICKEBUSCH.	
9th. St Eloi	Relieved 4th Rifle Brigade in trenches at St Eloi	4 men killed & 4 wounded
10th. St Eloi	In trenches at St Eloi	3 men killed & 4 wounded
11th. St Eloi	Relieved in trenches by 1st Royal Irish Regt; and marched back to DICKEBUSCH where Battalion bivouaced until following morning. Were shelled heavily during the day especially in 1.5, 16 & 2nd men killed	6 killed, 9 wounded
12th. WESTOUTRE	Marched early in morning to WESTOUTRE & were billeted there.	
13th. WESTOUTRE	Rested in billets at WESTOUTRE.	
14th. WESTOUTRE	Called out about 4 p.m. and marched to DICKEBUSCH from there to St Eloi to take part in counter attack	

WAR DIARY
or
INTELLIGENCE SUMMARY

(Erase heading not required.)

Army Form C. 2118.

Instructions regarding War Diaries and Intelligence Summaries are contained in F.S. Regs., Part II. and the Staff Manual respectively. Title pages will be prepared in manuscript.

Hour, Date, Place	Summary of Events and Information	Remarks and references to Appendices
MARCH 1914		
15th St ELOI and DICKEBUSCH	Early morning two companies under Major J. H. Bisley took part in the General attack on the mound ST ELOI. Returned to DICKEBUSCH about 9 a.m.	Captain C. M. VASSAR-SMITH killed, 2nd Lieut ? Bisley, 2 men ? ? (Killed), 3 wounded
16th DICKEBUSCH	Relieved L, E, F, G, in trenches at ST ELOI, Battalion 8 mi NE of Smith from ST ELOI moved by Royal Irish Regt; casualty wounded in leg.	1 man wounded
17th ST ELOI	In trenches at ST ELOI	
18th ST ELOI		
19th DICKEBUSCH	Relieved in trenches by 4th Rifle Brigade marched back to DICKEBUSCH	1 killed 1 died of wounds Lieut ZATORSKY D.C. wounded 2 killed + 3 wounded
20th ST ELOI	Battalion engaged in digging trenches at night at ST ELOI	
21/22 ST ELOI	Relieved 4th Rifle Brigade in St Eloi trenches. Battalion HdQrs in dug out YORKFIELD	4 wounded
22nd KRUISSTRAATHOEK	In trenches at ST ELOI	6 wounded
23rd DICKEBUSCH	Relieved in trenches by 4th Rifle Brigade and marched to the "Chateau" KROISSTRAATHOEK, 2 Ulhamheic ? billeted in DICKEBUSCH	6 wounded
24th DICKEBUSCH	Relieved at "Chateau" by 3rd K.R.R.C's and marched to DICKEBUSCH at billets	1 wounded
25th		
26th RENINGHELST	In billets Battalion lectured on Company drill,	
27th	Machine Gun Class & Bomb & Grenade throwing	
28th		
29th		
30th RENINGHELST	Battalion inspected by Corps Commander Lieut-General Sir H. Plumer	
31st RENINGHELST	Brigade inspected by Army Commander General Sir H.L. Smith-Dorrien.	

M.V.B.S.M.
4/15

Kennedy
Lieut Col.
Commanding 2nd Kings Liverpool LS

80th Infantry Brigade.
27th Division.

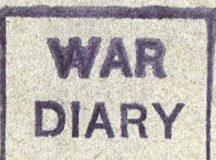

2nd BATTN. THE KING'S SHROPSHIRE LIGHT INFANTRY.

A P R I L

1 9 1 5

Army Form C. 2118.

WAR DIARY
or
INTELLIGENCE SUMMARY
(Erase heading not required.)

Instructions regarding War Diaries and Intelligence Summaries are contained in F.S. Regs., Part II. and the Staff Manual respectively. Title pages will be prepared in manuscript.

80/27

2 KSLI

Hour, Date, Place	Summary of Events and Information	Remarks and references to Appendices
APRIL 1915		
1st 2nd 3rd 4th RENINGHELST	In Billets Battalion exercised in Company Drill and Musketry.	
5th RENINGHELST	Battalion left RENINGHELST and marched to YPRES via VLAMERTINGHE	
6th YPRES	Billets at YPRES. Lt COLLINS joined Battalion	
7th YPRES	Relieved ARGYLE + SUTHERLAND Highlanders and 2nd FRENCH INFANTRY Regt in trenches.	
8th YPRES	In trenches.	1 man killed
9th YPRES	Relieved in trenches by 1st KRRC and 4th KRRC & 6yds East in support at LES ETRANGE DE BELLEWAERDE	LT.C. HOLMAN hit by Lt. A.J.B. LLOYD slightly wounded. 5 men killed wounded.
10th YPRES	In billets at YPRES.	
11th YPRES	Relieved 3rd KRRC & 4th KRRC in trenches at POLYGON WOOD	
12th POLYGON WOOD	In trenches at POLYGON WOOD	18 killed 9 wounded
13th POLYGON WOOD	In trenches at POLYGON WOOD	2 killed 7 wounded
14th POLYGON WOOD	Relieved in trenches by 1st KRRC and 4th KRRC.	
15th YPRES	In billets at YPRES	
16th YPRES	In billets at YPRES.	
17th YPRES	Battalion ordered to relieve 3rd KRRC and 4th KRRC in trenches in POLYGON WOOD	CAPT F. LENCH wounded Lt D BELL PAMS slightly wounded 1 man slightly wounded

Army Form C. 2118.

WAR DIARY
or
INTELLIGENCE SUMMARY
(Erase heading not required.)

Instructions regarding War Diaries and Intelligence Summaries are contained in F.S. Regs., Part II. and the Staff Manual respectively. Title pages will be prepared in manuscript.

Hour, Date, Place	Summary of Events and Information	Remarks and references to Appendices
APRIL 1915		
18th POLYGON WOOD	In trenches in POLYGON WOOD	1 Lieut.
19th POLYGON WOOD	In trenches in POLYGON WOOD. Commencement of shelling of YPRES by enemy.	
20th POLYGON WOOD	Battalion moved to @ of Bats BELLE-WARDE WOOD, being relieved by 2nd and 4th R.R.C. in support	
21st BELLEWARDE WOOD	2 Buffs bats BELLE-WARDE WOOD.	
22nd BELLEWARDE WOOD	Two Companies at 8pm ordered to G.H.Q. Line POTIJZE	
23rd POTIJZE	In G.H.Q. Line. Battalion less 1 Company acting as Divisional Reserve	No. 424 K146
24th POTIJZE	Early evening Battalion less 2 Coy to POLYGON WOOD returned to BELLEWARDE WOOD. less 1 Platoon	W 3 L 3
26th BELLEWARDE WOOD	At 9am Battalion marched to VERLORENHOEK. 1 Platoon BELLE-WARDE WOOD. Spent day in small dugs about 8pm 2 Companies ordered to retake trench lost by E.Surrey Regt. on previous day	
26th N. of POTIJZE	Battalion ordered to line a ridge N. of POTIJZE. about 10 am. By 3pm. advance was ordered, and found no enemy own ridge. Battalion spent night in ZEVE-COTE.	Lt BIDDLE COR?? Kelle CAPT HQ BRYANT 3 killed Lt BLAKEY ? Lt EVANS. 9 killed + miss. Bullets 25 wounded CAPT BATTYE wounded Lt BERDON + COLLINS wounded 4 NCOs + men killed +37 wounded Lt LLOYD Lt VOLECKER missing Lt WAGNER wounded 20 NCOs and men killed 78 - - - wounded
27th ZONNEBEKE	Ordered to retake lost trenches on enemy. Attack carried out at dawn was unsuccessful. Retired on ZEVECOTEN.	

12:17 W.3259 200,000 (E) 8/14 J.R.C.& A. Forms/C. 2118/11.

Army Form C. 2118.

WAR DIARY
or
INTELLIGENCE SUMMARY

(Erase heading not required.)

Instructions regarding War Diaries and Intelligence Summaries are contained in F.S. Regs., Part II. and the Staff Manual respectively. Title pages will be prepared in manuscript.

Hour, Date, Place	Summary of Events and Information	Remarks and references to Appendices
28. BELLEWARDE WOOD	Quarry day returned to BELLEWARDE WOOD, under orders of 80 BRIGADE	
29. BELLEWARDE WOOD	Day spent in support dug outs at BELLEWARDE WOOD	
30. BELLEWARDE WOOD	In support dug outs in BELLEWARDE WOOD + POLYGON WOOD. Lieut M.K. TURNER and GM.DLOW joined Battalion for duty.	

80th Infantry Brigade.
27th Division.

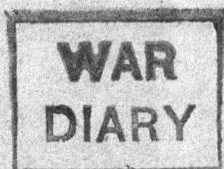

2nd BATTN. THE KING'S SHROPSHIRE LIGHT INFANTRY.

M A Y

1 9 1 5

Army Form C. 2118.

WAR DIARY
or
INTELLIGENCE SUMMARY
(Erase heading not required.)

2 WSLI

Instructions regarding War Diaries and Intelligence Summaries are contained in F. S. Regs., Part II. and the Staff Manual respectively. Title pages will be prepared in manuscript.

Hour, Date, Place	Summary of Events and Information	Remarks and references to Appendices
MAY 1915		
MAY 1st BELLEWARDE	In support dug outs BELLEWARDE WOOD. Digging trenches all night.	
2nd BELLEWARDE	In support in BELLEWARDE WOOD. Digging trenches at night.	
3rd BELLEWARDE	In support. Battalion moved to and occupied H.Q. line near POTIJZE	
4th POTIJZE	Battalion relieved R.D.F. & in trenches at BELLE WARDE WOOD	
5th BELLEWARDE	Trenches very heavily shelled. Enemy occupied two hills	LT TURNER slightly wounded 29 N.C.O. & men killed 51 N.C.O. & men wounded
6th BELLEWARDE	Battalion relieved in trenches by R.D.F. & and proceeded to S.H.Q. line	10 + 60. and men wounded once wounded 12 + 480. and men killed + wounded
7th POTIJZE		
8th POTIJZE	Battalion found working party 200 strong for repair of H.Q. line. Trenches heavily shelled. 2 companies sent in BELLE- WARDE LAKE. Two companies to fill up J.F. between 27 + 28 Divisions	LT.COL. BRIDGFORD wounded LT.& W. SHAW wounded LT. HALL wounded 10 killed 36 wounded LT. H. BERGER wounded 20 killed and wounded
9th RAILWAY WOOD	Trenches heavily shelled.	

J.A. Bailey Major
Comd 2 K.S.L.I.

Army Form C. 2118.

WAR DIARY
or
INTELLIGENCE SUMMARY

(Erase heading not required.)

Instructions regarding War Diaries and Intelligence Summaries are contained in F. S. Regs., Part II. and the Staff Manual respectively. Title pages will be prepared in manuscript.

Hour, Date, Place	Summary of Events and Information	Remarks and references to Appendices
MAY 1915		
10th RAILWAY WOOD	Shelled heavily shelled at day break. Cap'ns ROWAN-ROBINSON and C.R. WILKINSON, Lt. Hemsley joined Battalion in evening. Enemy heavily shelled.	20 killed and Wounded
11th RAILWAY WOOD		10 killed and Wounded
12 RAILWAY WOOD	Enemy intermittently shelling. Heavy shelling in evening by 6" batty. Dugouts went into bivouac ½ mile S.E. of VLAMERTINGHE J.N.B.	MAJOR ROWAN-ROBINSON MAJOR WILKINSON killed 12 killed and wounded
13th VLAMERTINGHE (1½ miles S. East of)	In bivouac. Draft of 97 of 6 D's and men arrived. 2nd Lt. J.S.H. BEAMISH & J.C.F. LISTER joined. In bivouac.	
14th VLAMERTINGHE (1½ miles S. East of) 15th VLAMERTINGHE (1½ miles S.E. of)	In bivouac. Battalion ordered to relieve 1st & K.R.R. in trenches nr BELLEWARDE LAKE.	
16th BELLEWARDE LAKE	In trenches near BELLEWARDE LAKE. Draft of 130 N.C.O. and men arrived.	7 killed 11 Wounded
17th BELLEWARDE LAKE	In trenches at BELLEWARDE LAKE. Relieved by 6 Dragoons. Marched to bivouac at BUSSE BOOM.	1 killed 6 wounded

J. A. Bailey Major
Comdg. YKLIO

Army Form C. 2118.

WAR DIARY
or
INTELLIGENCE SUMMARY

(Erase heading not required.)

Instructions regarding War Diaries and Intelligence Summaries are contained in F. S. Regs., Part II. and the Staff Manual respectively. Title pages will be prepared in manuscript.

Hour, Date, Place	Summary of Events and Information	Remarks and references to Appendices
MAY 1915		
18th BUSSEBOOM	In bivouac at BUSSEBOOM.	
19th BUSSEBOOM	In bivouac at BUSSEBOOM.	
20th BUSSEBOOM	In bivouac. Battalion inspected by Sir J. French.	
21st BUSSEBOOM	In bivouac. Draft of 130 N.C.O's and men joined the Battalion. Lieut. R. M. Robinson and Lieut. R. A. L. PERSSE joined Battalion.	
22nd BUSSEBOOM	In bivouac.	
23rd BUSSEBOOM	In bivouac. Captain D. Leslie joined Battalion.	
24th BUSSEBOOM	In bivouac. Battalion orders to move at 5.10 a.m. on account of 28th Division and right of 4 & 6 Division being forced. At past 5.30 p.m. Battalion was ordered to relieve trenches in vicinity of BELLEWAARDE LAKE which had been lost by 28th Division. Orders moved along YPRES - ROULERS railway and took up position in and in rear of G.H.Q. Line.	

J. H. Reilly Major
Comdg YK. S. L. ?

Army Form C. 2118.

WAR DIARY
or
INTELLIGENCE SUMMARY

(Erase heading not required.)

Instructions regarding War Diaries and Intelligence Summaries are contained in F. S. Regs., Part II. and the Staff Manual respectively. Title pages will be prepared in manuscript.

Hour, Date, Place	Summary of Events and Information	Remarks and references to Appendices
MAY 1915		
8 p.m. YPRES	About 1 a.m. Battalion was ordered to advance and attack enemy's trenches in vicinity of BELLEWARDE FARM. Attack failed. Battalion held line of trees west of WHITTPORT FARM and entrenched itself.	2LT. STEWARD) Killed 2LT. HAZARD) CAPT. LESLIE, LTs, WILLIAMS-FREEMAN, LISTER, BEAMISH, MAIDLOW, ROBINSON, Wounded. 192 Other Ranks, Killed, wounded and missing.
26th WHITTPORT FARM	In new line of trenches. Stay Pouring night. Battalion relieved on evening and went into bivouac at BUSSE BOOM.	
27. BUSSE BOOM	In bivouac. 2LT. F.S.D. Hill and J. BEEDE'S joined Battalion.	
28. BUSSE BOOM	In bivouac. Lt. Bn. Allenby joined 1st army corps worker Battalion. 3d @ rank of 2d N.C.O. and men joined Battalion.	
29. BUSSE BOOM	In bivouac. 2LT. F.L.M. GRIVER and 2LTABS. MOHN joined Battalion.	
30. BUSSE BOOM	In bivouac. Brigade ordered to move about 9 at midnight @ orders received from Battn of Sea Boys. Proceed to ARMENTIERES, which @ orders received from BRANDEURS.	
31st BUSSE BOOM	At 1.30 am marched and bivouacked at BRANDEURS, arriving there about 7 a.m.	

J.H. Bailey Major
Comdy. 1K.L.L.R.

80th Infantry Brigade.
27th Division.

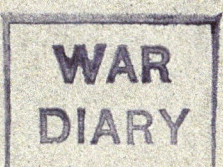

2nd BATTN. THE KING'S SHROPSHIRE LIGHT INFANTRY.

J U N E

1 9 1 5

WAR DIARY or INTELLIGENCE SUMMARY

Army Form C. 2118.

2 WSLI
2 KRRC

Hour, Date, Place	Summary of Events and Information	Remarks and references to Appendices
JUNE 1915		
1st DRANOUTRE	Marched with Brigade at 11.0am to STEENWERCK. 2nd Lts A.A. TIPPET and H. GRUBB on joining Battalion.	
2nd STEENWERCK	Marched with Brigade at 11pm to ARMENTIERES. Relieved N. STAFFORD REGT in trenches.	1 wounded
3rd ARMENTIERES	In trenches at ARMENTIERES	2 killed and 10 wounded
4th ARMENTIERES	In trenches at ARMENTIERES	1 wounded
5th ARMENTIERES	In trenches. Battalion relieved in evening by 3/KRRC and 4/KRB. LT. R.ST.V. RICHARDS (3rd S.R Bn) joined Battalion	
6th ARMENTIERES	In billets at ARMENTIERES. 2nd Lts J.K LLOYD, T. WOOD, C.P. HAZARD joined from 3rd S.R Battalion.	
7th ARMENTIERES	In billets	
8th ARMENTIERES	In billets. 2nd Lt. A.S. ASBURY (3/KRRC) and 2nd Lt. V. C. W. BENNETT joined Battalion. Relieved 4/K.R.R.B. in trenches in evening.	1 killed 3 wounded
9th ARMENTIERES	In trenches	1 killed
10th ARMENTIERES	In trenches	

J. H. Bailey Major
Commdg 2/K.R.R.C

Army Form C. 2118.

WAR DIARY
or
INTELLIGENCE SUMMARY

(Erase heading not required.)

Instructions regarding War Diaries and Intelligence Summaries are contained in F. S. Regs., Part II. and the Staff Manual respectively. Title pages will be prepared in manuscript.

Hour, Date, Place	Summary of Events and Information	Remarks and references to Appendices
JUNE 1915		
11th ARMENTIERES	In trenches. Draft of 79 Other Ranks joined Battalion and occupied support trenches. Lieut. R.A. HARGREAVE (2Lt) and 2 Lt R.M. WARLOW joined Battalion.	1 Wounded.
12th ARMENTIERES	In trenches	
13th ARMENTIERES	In trenches	2 Wounded.
14th ARMENTIERES	In trenches. Bombardment released in reply to 4/8.03am	1 killed 1 Wounded
15th ⎫ ARMENTIERES		
16th ⎬	In billets. Lieuts. MR KOCK, J.B. PAYNE, R.A. ELDER, H.R. BOOTH joined Battalion from 28th Batn. of LONDON REGT. on 16" - Battalion relieved WIKPRS and PR.R'S in trenches on evening of 17"	
17th ⎭		
18th ⎫		
19th ⎬		
20th ⎪ ARMENTIERES	In trenches	3 Wounded
21st ⎨		1 Wounded
22nd ⎪		1 Killed 2 Wounded
23rd ⎭		1 Killed
24th ARMENTIERES	In trenches. Relieved by WIKPRG.	

J.A. Bailey Major
Comdg. 7/K.L.R.

Army Form C. 2118.

WAR DIARY
or
INTELLIGENCE SUMMARY

(Erase heading not required.)

Instructions regarding War Diaries and Intelligence Summaries are contained in F. S. Regs., Part II. and the Staff Manual respectively. Title pages will be prepared in manuscript.

Hour, Date, Place	Summary of Events and Information	Remarks and references to Appendices
JUNE 1916		
25th ARMENTIÈRES	In billets. Capt R E HOLMES à COURT from 2nd (R.R.) Bn and 2nd LT H.P. BEARDON (D.L.I.) from hospital join Bn Battalion.	
26th ARMENTIÈRES	In Billets.	
27th ARMENTIÈRES	In Billets. Relieved 9th R. Scots in trenches.	
28th ARMENTIÈRES	In trenches	S. of Houplines
29th ARMENTIÈRES	In trenches. 2nd Lt P. THORNE-WAITE joins Battalion from 2.9. CITY OF LONDON Regt	
30th ARMENTIÈRES	In trenches.	

J.H. Bailey Major
Comdg. 7th Shropos L.I.

80th Infantry Brigade.
27th Division.

WAR DIARY

2nd BATTN. THE KING'S SHROPSHIRE LIGHT INFANTRY.

J U L Y

1 9 1 5

80th Infantry Brigade.
27th Division.

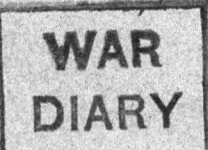
WAR DIARY

2nd BATTN. THE KING'S SHROPSHIRE LIGHT INFANTRY.

J U L Y

1 9 1 5

Army Form C. 2118.

WAR DIARY
or
INTELLIGENCE SUMMARY

(Erase heading not required.)

Instructions regarding War Diaries and Intelligence Summaries are contained in F. S. Regs., Part II. and the Staff Manual respectively. Title pages will be prepared in manuscript.

Hour, Date, Place	Summary of Events and Information	Remarks and references to Appendices
JULY		
1st ARMENTIERES	Relieved (less 1 Coy) in trenches by 3/E.R.R.C. & 4/R.Sussex. Went into billets in ARMENTIERES.	Capt. R.E. HOLMES à COURT, 2nd Lt. J.M.L. GROVER, C.P. HAZARD, V.R. BOOTH. 5 O.R.'s and 3 Other Ranks wounded by a shell when parading in the street.
2nd ARMENTIERES	In billets.	
3rd ARMENTIERES	In billets. 1 Coy in support trenches relieved by another Company in support trenches.	
4th ARMENTIERES	In billets.	
5th ARMENTIERES	In billets. Battalion relieved 2/R.Berks and 1/R.E.R.I. in trenches in evening.	
6th ARMENTIERES	In trenches.	1 Other Rank wounded.
7th ARMENTIERES	In trenches.	1 Other Rank wounded.
8th ARMENTIERES	In trenches.	1 Other Rank killed 1 Wd.
9th ARMENTIERES	In trenches. Battalion less one Company in support trenches relieved by 3/K.R.R.C.	2nd Lt. A.M. WARLOW wounded. 5 Other Ranks wounded.

8/10/15. J.H. Barlow Lt. Colonel
Comdg. 4th A.L.2

Army Form C. 2118.

WAR DIARY
or
INTELLIGENCE SUMMARY

(Erase heading not required.)

Instructions regarding War Diaries and Intelligence Summaries are contained in F. S. Regs., Part II. and the Staff Manual respectively. Title pages will be prepared in manuscript.

Hour, Date, Place JULY	Summary of Events and Information	Remarks and references to Appendices
10th ARMENTIÈRES	In billets in ARMENTIÈRES	1 Other Rank Wounded.
11th ARMENTIÈRES	In billets. A company relieved company in support trenches in evening.	1 Other Rank Killed.
12th ARMENTIÈRES	In billets.	1 Other Rank Wounded.
13th ARMENTIÈRES	In billets. Battalion relieved 1/8. K.R.R.C. in trenches.	
14th ARMENTIÈRES	In trenches. Town of ARMENTIÈRES heavily shelled during day.	
15th ARMENTIÈRES	In trenches.	1 Other Rank Killed. 1 Woman.
16th ARMENTIÈRES	In trenches.	2 Other Ranks Wounded.
17th ARMENTIÈRES	In trenches. Battalion relieved in evening by 9th and 6/8 D.L.I. and marched to bivouac in fields near STEENWERCK	
18th to 31st STEENWERCK	In bivouac.	

8/10/15
J. H. Bailey Lt. Colonel
Comdt. 4th Kings Shropshire L.I.

1247 W 3299 200,000 (E) 8/14 J.B.C. & A. Forms/C. 2118/11.

80th Infantry Brigade.
27th Division.

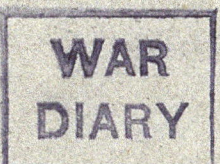

2nd BATTN. THE KING'S SHROPSHIRE LIGHT INFANTRY.

A U G U S T

1 9 1 5

80th Infantry Brigade.

27th Division.

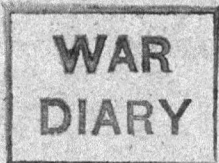

2nd BATTN. THE KING'S SHROPSHIRE LIGHT INFANTRY.

A U G U S T

1 9 1 5

Army Form C. 2118.

WAR DIARY
or
INTELLIGENCE SUMMARY
(Erase heading not required.)

Instructions regarding War Diaries and Intelligence Summaries are contained in F. S. Regs., Part II. and the Staff Manual respectively. Title pages will be prepared in manuscript.

Hour, Date, Place	Summary of Events and Information	Remarks and references to Appendices
AUGUST		
1st STEENWERCK	In bivouac. 6 Officers + all by comds visited new trenches	1 O.Ranks Missing believed killed, reconnoitring party.
2nd STEENWERCK	Battalion was to occupy. In bivouac. Battalion relieved the 2nd Gloucester Regt in trenches in evening	
3rd. BOIS GRENIER	In trenches	2 O. Ranks wounded.
4th. BOIS GRENIER	In trenches.	2 O. Ranks wounded
5th. BOIS GRENIER	In trenches	1 O. Rank killed. 1 Wounded.
6th. BOIS GRENIER	In trenches	2 O. Ranks Wounded
7th. BOIS GRENIER	In trenches.	
8th. BOIS GRENIER	In trenches.	
9th BOIS GRENIER	In trenches. Battalion relieved in evening by 4th Bde. and went into bivouacs at GRIS-POT	
10th GRIS-POT	In bivouac.	
11th GRIS-POT	In bivouac.	
12th GRIS-POT	In bivouac.	

J. A. Purley Lt Colonel
g/o/c 2 South Staffs Drops L.I

1247 W 8299 200,000 (E) 8/14 J.B.C. & A. Forms/C. 2118/11.

Army Form C. 2118.

WAR DIARY
or
INTELLIGENCE SUMMARY
(Erase heading not required.)

Instructions regarding War Diaries and Intelligence Summaries are contained in F. S. Regs., Part II. and the Staff Manual respectively. Title pages will be prepared in manuscript.

Hour, Date, Place	Summary of Events and Information	Remarks and references to Appendices
AUGUST		
13th GRIS-PÔT	In bivouac. Bivouac area shelled by enemy.	1 O. Rank slightly wounded.
14th GRIS-PÔT	Lt. Col: R. J. Bradford appointed Brig: Gen: to 18th Infy Bde. In bivouac. Battalion commanded by Major J. B. Bailey vice Lt. Col. Bradford.	
15th GRIS-PÔT	In bivouac.	
16th GRIS-PÔT	In bivouac. Battalion relieved 1 R. Ber in trenches	1 O.Rank slightly wounded.
17th BOIS GRENIER	In trenches.	1 O. Rank slightly wounded.
18th BOIS GRENIER	In trenches.	3 O. Ranks slightly wounded. 2nd Lt. A. H. Tupper, killed
19th BOIS GRENIER	In trenches.	1 O. Rank wounded.
20th BOIS GRENIER	In trenches.	2 O. Ranks wounded.
21st BOIS GRENIER	In trenches.	
22nd BOIS GRENIER	In trenches.	1 O. Rank killed, 1 wounded.
23rd BOIS GRENIER	In trenches. Battalion was relieved in evening by 1/R. Ber	4 O. Ranks wounded
	1 Boy Company in support trenches, and went into bivouac at GRIS-PÔT as Bgde Reserve.	
25th GRIS-PÔT	In bivouac. Major b. W. Battie D.S.O. and Captain J. A. Henriot joined Battalion.	4 O. Ranks wounded.

8/10/15 J. H. Bailey Lt. Colonel
1/10/15 2d Comdg. Yorks & Lancs L. D

Army Form C. 2118.

WAR DIARY
or
INTELLIGENCE SUMMARY

(Erase heading not required.)

Instructions regarding War Diaries and Intelligence Summaries are contained in F. S. Regs, Part II. and the Staff Manual respectively. Title pages will be prepared in manuscript.

Hour, Date, Place	Summary of Events and Information	Remarks and references to Appendices
AUGUST		
25th GRIS-PÔT	In bivouac.	
26th GRIS-PÔT	In bivouac.	
27th GRIS-PÔT	In bivouac.	
28th GRIS-PÔT	In bivouac.	
29th GRIS-PÔT	In bivouac.	
30th GRIS-PÔT	In bivouac. Battalion relieved from Brigade Reserve by 2nd Bn Royal Irish Fusiliers, and moved into bivouac at HALLOBEAU joining Divisional Reserve.	
31st GRIS-PÔT	In bivouac.	

J. H. Kelly, Lt Colonel
Comdg. 9th R.Irish Rifles L.I.
8/19/15

80th Infantry Brigade.
27th Division.

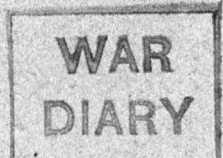

2nd BATTN. THE KING'S SHROPSHIRE LIGHT INFANTRY.

S E P T E M B E R

1 9 1 5

Army Form C. 2118.

WAR DIARY
or
INTELLIGENCE SUMMARY

(Erase heading not required.)

Instructions regarding War Diaries and Intelligence Summaries are contained in F. S. Regs., Part II. and the Staff Manual respectively. Title pages will be prepared in manuscript.

Hour, Date, Place		Summary of Events and Information	Remarks and references to Appendices
SEPTEMBER			
1st	HALLOBEAU	In billets	
2nd	HALLOBEAU	In billets	
3rd	HALLOBEAU	In billets	
4th	HALLOBEAU	In billets. Draft of 40 Other Ranks joined Battalion	1 Other Rank slightly ill.
5th	HALLOBEAU	In billets	
6th	HALLOBEAU	In billets	
7th	HALLOBEAU	In billets	
8th	HALLOBEAU	In billets. Draft of 30 Other Ranks joined Battalion	
9th	HALLOBEAU	In billets	
10th	HALLOBEAU	In billets	
11th	HALLOBEAU	In billets	
12th	HALLOBEAU	In billets. Hostile aeroplane brought down near billets.	
13th	HALLOBEAU	In billets. Battalion left HALLOBEAU at 6.15 pm & marched to STEENWERCK where Battalion concentrated. Brigade marched at 1.30 am via MERRIS—STRAZEELE and Battalion bivouacked at BORRE.	
14th	HALLOBEAU	In bivouac.	
15th	BORRE	In bivouac. 80th Brigade inspected by 2nd Corps Commander. Battalion paraded at 4.15 am and marched to HAZEBROUCK where it entrained for OUILLACOURT, arrived OUILLACOURT at 6.30 pm. Bussed in Motor buses to MERRICOURT and marched to FROISSY arriving at 10.30 pm. Billeted on farms by SOMME canal for night.	
16th	BORRE		
17th	BORRE		
18th	BORRE		

J. H. Bailey, Lt. Colonel
13/9/16 L. Bondy ?? Y. L. J.

Army Form C. 2118.

WAR DIARY
or
INTELLIGENCE SUMMARY

(Erase heading not required.)

Instructions regarding War Diaries and Intelligence Summaries are contained in F. S. Regs., Part II. and the Staff Manual respectively. Title pages will be prepared in manuscript.

Hour, Date, Place	Summary of Events and Information	Remarks and references to Appendices
SEPTEMBER		
19th FROISSY	One killed. Battalion forward at 9pm and marched to CAPPY arriving at 4.30am and bivouacked for night in fields outside village.	
20th CAPPY	In bivouac. Battalion relieved 125th French Infantry Regiment in trenches in evening.	
21st CAPPY	In trenches	1 O. Rank Wounded
22nd CAPPY	In trenches	2nd Lt. M.P. ROCH killed.
23rd CAPPY	In trenches	2 O. Ranks Wounded
24th CAPPY	In trenches	
25th CAPPY	In trenches. Battalion relieved in evening by 4/R. Berks. and went into billets in CAPPY.	1 O. Rank slightly wounded
26th CAPPY		
27th CAPPY		
28th CAPPY	One killed	
29th CAPPY		
30th CAPPY		

J. A. Bailey Lt. Colonel
Commdg. 7th Bn Oxfords L.I.

80th Infantry Brigade.
27th Division.

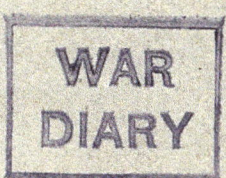

2nd BATTN. THE KING'S SHROPSHIRE LIGHT INFANTRY.

OCTOBER

1915

80th Infantry Brigade.
27th Division.

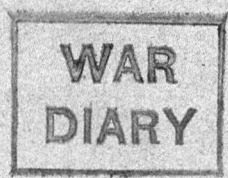

2nd BATTN. THE KING'S SHROPSHIRE LIGHT INFANTRY.

OCTOBER

1915

Army Form C. 2118

WAR DIARY
or
INTELLIGENCE SUMMARY
(Erase heading not required.)

Instructions regarding War Diaries and Intelligence Summaries are contained in F. S. Regs., Part II. and the Staff Manual respectively. Title Pages will be prepared in manuscript.

Place	Date	Hour	Summary of Events and Information	Remarks and references to Appendices
CAPPY	1-10-15		In billets at Cappy. Relieved 4/R.Bde. in the trenches.	
CAPPY	2-10-15		In trenches.	Casualties Nil
CAPPY	3-10-15		In trenches.	Casualties Nil
CAPPY	4-10-15		In trenches.	
CAPPY	5-10-15		In trenches. Capt F.R.MAUNSELL. and 4 O.R. slightly wounded.	
			Battalion relieved in trenches by 4/R.Bde. and went into billets at FROISSY.	
			Lieut: V.H.Crane. rejoined Battalion from 3rd Battalion.	
FROISSY	6-10-15		In billets	
FROISSY	7-10-15		In billets	
FROISSY	8-10-15		In billets	
FROISSY	9-10-15		In billets. Relieved 5/R.Bde. in trenches in evening	
CAPPY	10-10-15		In trenches	
CAPPY	11-10-15		In trenches	
CAPPY	12-10-15		In trenches	
CAPPY	13-10-15		In trenches. Battalion relieved in evening by 4/R.Bde. Went into billets in CAPPY. I.O.R.Hilles	

J.A.Bailey Lt.Col
19/11/15
Cmdg 9th R.I.

Army Form C. 2118

WAR DIARY
or
INTELLIGENCE SUMMARY
(Erase heading not required.)

Instructions regarding War Diaries and Intelligence Summaries are contained in F. S. Regs., Part II. and the Staff Manual respectively. Title Pages will be prepared in manuscript.

Place	Date	Hour	Summary of Events and Information	Remarks and references to Appendices
CAPPY	14/9/15		In billets	
CAPPY	15/9/15		In billets	
CAPPY	16/9/15		In billets. Battalion relieved in billets by 2nd Camerons and marched to MORCOURT via MERICOURT.	
MORCOURT	17/9/15		In billets	
MORCOURT	18/9/15		In billets	
MORCOURT	19/9/15		In billets	
MORCOURT	20/9/15		In billets. Battalion ordered to relieve 7th S.W.B. in trenches. Battalion marches at 3.40pm via MERICOURT and CAPPY to trenches and relieves 7 SWB	
CAPPY	21/9/15		In Trenches	
CAPPY	22/9/15		In Trenches. Battalion relieved in evening by 4th R.Rif. and went into billets in CAPPY	
CAPPY	23/9/15		In billets	
CAPPY	24/9/15		In billets	

19/11 J.R. Bailey Lt Col
/15 Comdg 7th S.L.R.?

1875 Wt. W593/826 1,000,000 4/15 J.B.C. & A. A.D.S.S./Forms/C. 2118.

Army Form C. 2118

WAR DIARY
or
INTELLIGENCE SUMMARY

(Erase heading not required.)

Instructions regarding War Diaries and Intelligence Summaries are contained in F. S. Regs., Part II. and the Staff Manual respectively. Title Pages will be prepared in manuscript.

Place	Date	Hour	Summary of Events and Information	Remarks and references to Appendices
CAPPY	25/10/15		In billets. Battalion relieved by 151st French Regt. paraded at 5 pm and marched to MERICOURT via FROISSY, and billeted at MERICOURT for night	
MERICOURT	26/10/15		Battalion paraded at 7 am and marched to ABANCOURT via MORCOURT arriving about 10.30 am. Billeted in ABANCOURT for night.	
ABANCOURT	27/10/15		Battalion paraded at 8.30 am. and marched to BOVES via VILLIERS-BRETON. NEAUX arriving about 1 pm In camp for night	
BOVES	28/10/15		Battalion struck Camp and paraded at 10.30 am and marched to PISSY via ST FUSCIEN, DURY, VERS, and CLAIRY.	
PISSY	29/10/15		In billets	
PISSY	30/10/15		In billets	
PISSY	31/10/15		In billets	

10/11/15

J. A. Baily Lt Col.
Comdg: 7th A. L. ?

1875 Wt. W593/826 1,000,000 4/15 J.B.C. & A. A.D.S.S./Forms/C. 2118.

www.ingramcontent.com/pod-product-compliance
Lightning Source LLC
Chambersburg PA
CBHW081246170426
43191CB00037B/2056